Usborne

Easy Piano Tunes

Anthony Marks

Designed and illustrated by Candice Whatmore

Edited by Kirsteen Rogers

Music selected, arranged and edited by Anthony Marks
New compositions by Anthony Marks
Piano adviser: John York
Music setting: Andrew Jones

Contents

About the music

The tunes in this book come from all over the world. You'll already know some of them, though others may be less familiar. There are nursery rhymes and folk tunes, Christmas carols and sea shanties as well as some famous pieces of classical music. Three of the pieces were written specially for this book. Most of the tunes weren't written for the piano originally and have been specially arranged for this book to make them easy to play on the piano. The pieces are roughly in order of difficulty so the hardest ones come at the end.

On each music page you'll find some information about the piece. If you find a word that you don't understand, look at the list of music words on page 64.

Internet links

If you have a computer, you can listen to all the pieces in this book on the Usborne Quicklinks Website to hear how they go. Just go to **www.usborne-quicklinks.com** and type in the keywords "easy piano", then follow the simple instructions.

Mary had a little lamb

This American nursery rhyme is said to tell a true story about a little girl named Mary Sawyer, who took her pet lamb to school. It has the same tune as an old song, "Merrily we roll along", but nobody is sure which came first.

On the riverbank

This is an old tune from eastern Europe. Play
it smoothly without gaps between the notes.
See if you think it sounds better fast or slow.

Gently

The grand old Duke of York

Like a march

This tune was written in the 18th century. The
Duke of York was the son of King George III of
England. He fought wars in France and Holland.

The knight's song

This is a very old French tune. There are lots of French songs about knights and castles that were written by wandering musicians called troubadours.

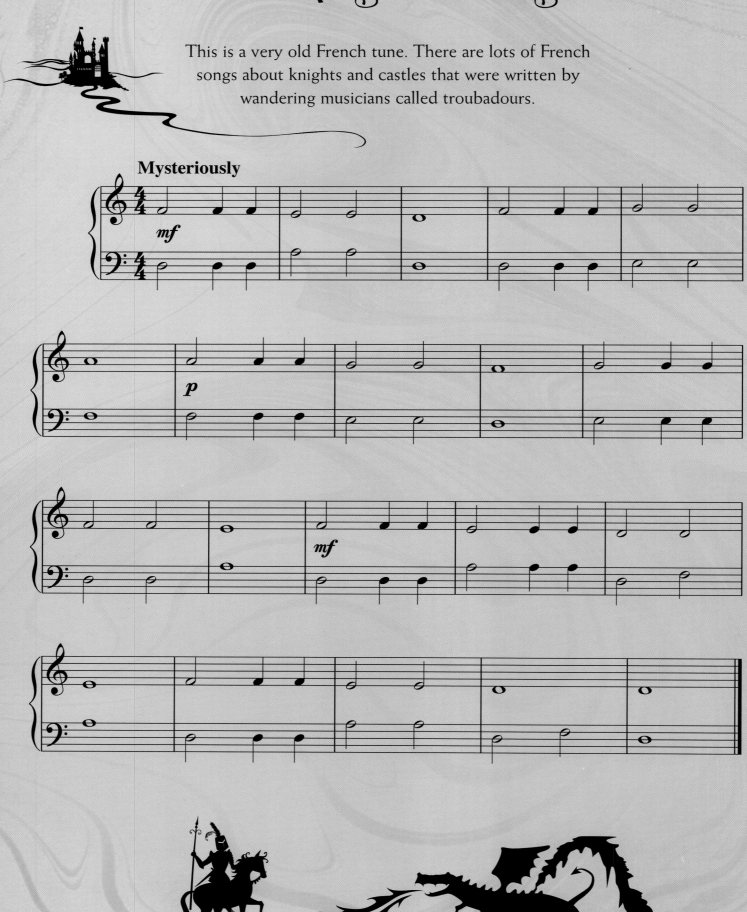

Bobby Shafto

"Bobby Shafto" was first sung in the north of England in the 18th century. It is about a sailor who goes away to sea.

London Bridge is falling down

The Romans first built London Bridge, probably out
of wood. It had to be rebuilt many times because
the River Thames kept sweeping it away.

Sur le pont d'Avignon

This is a French tune. The title means "On the bridge at Avignon", though people used to dance on an island in the river under the bridge, not on top of it.

Streets of Laredo

This is an old cowboy tune. Laredo is a city in
America, near the border between Texas and
Mexico. Watch out for the F sharps.

Gently and a bit sadly

Billy boy

This tune is now more popular in the USA, but was
probably first sung in Britain and taken to America in
the 18th or 19th century. Look out for the B flats.

Home on the range

This American song was written in the 1870s
by Brewster Higley and Daniel Kelley. It is
now the state song of Kansas.

Not too quickly

Where, oh where, has my little dog gone?

This tune was published in America in 1864 by the composer Septimus Winner. He based it on a German song about a man who loses his socks.

Silent night

"Silent night" was written in Oberndorf, Austria, by a teacher named Franz Gruber and a priest named Josef Mohr. It was first performed on Christmas Eve, 1818.

How far is it to Bethlehem?

Nobody knows who wrote this English
Christmas carol, but it is hundreds of
years old. Play it slowly and quietly.

Scarborough fair

This English tune was first sung in the Middle Ages.
Once a year there was a huge market and fair in
the seaside town of Scarborough.

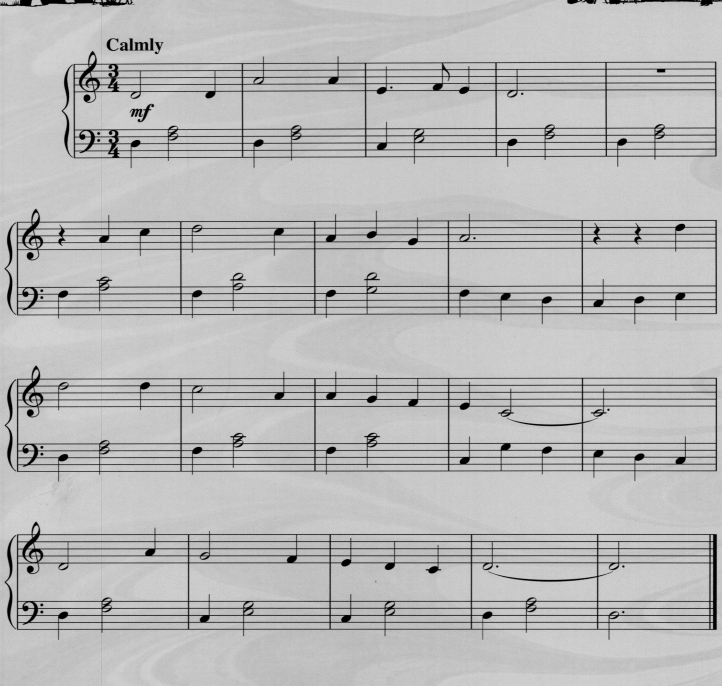

Lavender's blue

Andantino

This is a 17th-century English song. Lavender is a sweet-smelling plant. People believed it would help them sleep and give them pleasant dreams.

Frère Jacques

The title of this old French song means "Brother James". It is about a monk. Your two hands play the same tune, but not at the same time. This is called a round. The second half of the piece is a new tune that uses the same notes, but in reverse order.

Wake up!

Michael, row the boat ashore

This tune is a spiritual. Spirituals were first sung in
America in the early 19th century. For the left hand
part, think of a boat bobbing on water.

Turn the glasses over

This is a sailors' song called a sea shanty. "Shanty" comes from the French word "chanter", which means "to sing". Shanties were often about life at sea.

What shall we do with the drunken sailor?

Sailors sang shanties while they were doing hard work
such as pulling ropes. The rhythm of the music helped
them keep time, which made the work easier.

Land of the silver birch

This tune is from Canada.
Play it quite lightly and make sure
you don't rush the short notes.

Solemnly

The ash grove

"The ash grove" is a very old Welsh tune.
Watch out for the repeat and keep
the short notes steady.

Island song

This tune was written specially for this book.
Count the rests in the second half very carefully,
as some of them come in unexpected places.

Sweetly and smoothly

O my darling Clementine

This American song was written by Percy Montross around 1880.
It is about a gold-miner's family. In the late 1840s, gold was
discovered in California. In 1849, thousands of Americans moved
there, hoping to find gold. They were called the "Forty-niners".

Like a waltz

Donkey riding

This tune may have started out as a French sailors' song in
the 18th century. Later it became popular in Canada. The
title comes from the "donkey engine", a steam-powered
machine used to move logs.

Toreador's song

This music is from "Carmen", an opera by a French composer
named Georges Bizet. It was first performed in 1875. It is
about a woman who falls in love with a bullfighter.

The trout

Franz Schubert, an Austrian composer, wrote this
tune around 1817. Later he used it in a larger
piece for piano and four stringed instruments.

Daisy, Daisy

Harry Dacre, an English songwriter, wrote this in 1892.
It is about a couple being married and riding away
on a tandem (a bicycle for two people).

Happily

Ding dong! Merrily on high

Although this tune is best known as a Christmas
carol, it is a French dance from the 16th century.
Keep it steady, particularly in the second half.

O little town of Bethlehem

Nobody knows who wrote this English
Christmas carol, but it is hundreds of years old.
Play it quietly, like a lullaby.

Andante

Ma oz tsur

Jewish people sing this during Hanukkah, a winter festival.
The title means "Rock that shelters me".

Cockles and mussels

This was written in the 1880s by James Yorkston.
It is about Dublin, the capital city of Ireland, and
is sometimes known as "Molly Malone".

The Londonderry air

An Irish woman named Jane Ross first
wrote this tune down in the 1850s after
she heard it played by a local musician.

Slowly and sadly

The minstrel boy

Nobody knows who wrote this Irish tune, which is also called "The Moreen". It was first published in the 19th century with words by Thomas Moore, telling the story of a minstrel boy who goes to war.

Like a march

Snake in the grass

This tune was written specially for this book. Try
to make it sound very smooth and a little scary.
Be careful not to rush the shorter notes.

Greensleeves

Some people say King Henry VIII of England wrote this. No one knows exactly how it originally sounded. Once you've learned the music, you could play some of the circled note names instead of the written notes, and see which you like best.

Andantino

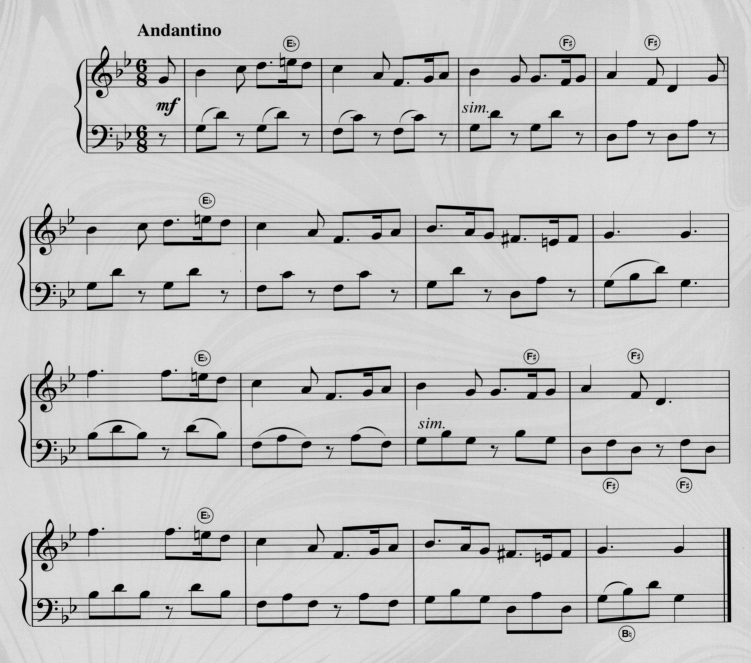

Waltzing Matilda

"Waltzing Matilda" is an Australian tune. It was written in 1895 by Banjo Patterson, though it is based on an older Scottish tune called "Craigielee".

The bear went over the mountain

This is an American tune from the 19th century.
It is also called "For he's a jolly good fellow".

Tingalayo

This is a Caribbean song about a
donkey. Play the rhythms evenly,
making them neat and precise.

Sing for me, little bird

"Sing for me, little bird" is based on a folk tune
from the Caribbean. Count very carefully and
make sure you don't rush the short notes.

Wedding march

A German composer, Felix
Mendelssohn, wrote this tune in 1843.
Watch out for the repeat.

D.S. al Fine

Nkosi sikelel iAfrika

The English title of this tune is "Lord, bless Africa".
It was written in 1897 by Enoch Sontonga, and is
now the national anthem of South Africa.

This train is bound for glory

Nobody knows who wrote this tune.
It is American and was probably first sung
in the 19th century.

Simple gifts

Joseph Brackett, a member of an American religious group called the Shakers, wrote this tune in 1848.

47

Les moissonneurs

François Couperin, a French composer, wrote this
piece in 1716, for an old keyboard instrument called
a harpsichord. The title means "The harvesters".

Rhythmic but not too quickly

f

tr **Fine**

mp

D.C. al Fine

Song of the reapers

This piece was written in 1848 by a German composer named Robert Schumann. It is one of a group of pieces for young people called "Album for the young".

Gently and evenly

Musette

This tune was written in the 18th century by
J.S. Bach, a German composer. It has a continuous
left-hand note called a drone. This imitates an old
instrument called a musette, which is a kind of bagpipe.

Moderato

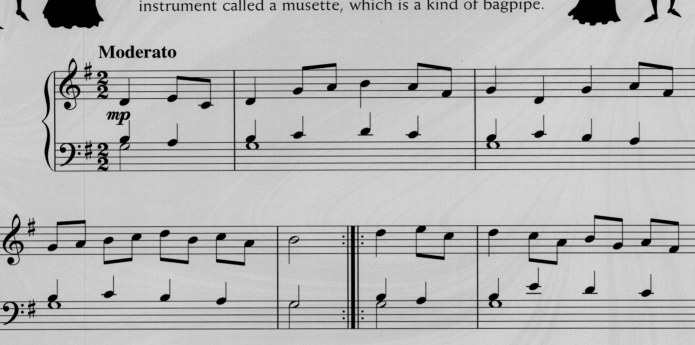

It was a lover and his lass

An English composer named Thomas Morley wrote this tune. It was published in 1600, and was also used in "As you like it", a play written by Shakespeare.

Jenny pluck pears

This piece is the tune to an old English dance. It was first published in a book called "The Dancing Master", which contains the tunes and steps for hundreds of country dances.

Delicately

Gathering peascods

Like the tune opposite, this tune appeared in
"The Dancing Master". It was published in 1651
by John Playford, a musician and bookseller
who lived in London.

The sailor woman

Nobody knows who wrote this tune. It was
first published in the 17th century in France,
but it is much older than that.

Two by two

This tune is also called "When Johnny comes
marching home". It was written by Patrick Gilmore,
an American bandmaster, in the 1860s.

55

Ma Normandie

A French songwriter, Frédéric Bérat, wrote this tune in 1836. Bérat was born in Rouen, a city in Normandy. Normandy is famous for its butter, milk and cheese.

Slowly and a bit sadly

Les trois rois

"Les trois rois" is a very old Christmas song from Provence
in the south of France. The title means "The three kings".
Play it like a march, with a very crisp rhythm.

O happy day!

This is an old song, but it was made famous
in the 1960s by the Edwin Hawkins Singers,
an American Gospel choir.

Joyfully and very rhythmic

Galway city

Galway is a city in the west of Ireland.
This tune was first published in 1624.
It is also known as "Spanish ladies".

Quickly and brightly

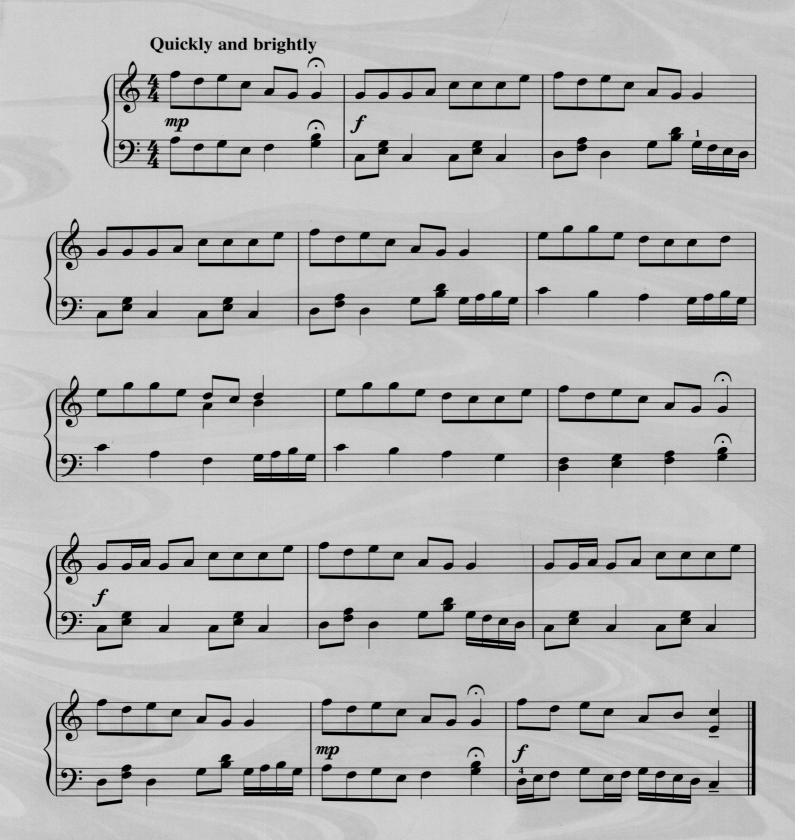

Hammer and tongs

This tune was written specially for this book.
Look out for the bars that you have to play
an octave higher than written.

60

The Arethusa

The Arethusa was an English battleship in the 18th century. This song was written in the 1790s by William Shield and Prince Hoare.

Shenandoah

Shenandoah was a native American chief who lived
by the Missouri River. The tune became popular in
the 1820s, but it may be older.

Go, tell it on the mountain

This tune was first sung by slaves in the southern
USA. It was published in 1907 by an African-
American composer, John Wesley Work.

Music words

Tempo instructions

Tempo instructions are often written at the start of a piece or section, to tell you how quickly or slowly to play. Other instructions in the music itself tell you the mood of the music, or which part of the piece to play next. Most of the ones in this book are in English, but some are in Italian. (Musicians use Italian words because music was first printed in Italy, hundreds of years ago.) This is what they mean:

Allegretto	fairly lively
Allegro	quickly
Allegro molto	very quickly
Andante	relaxed, at a walking pace
Andantino	a little faster than andante
D.C. al Fine	go back to the start and play to the "Fine" sign
D.S. al Fine	go back to the 𝄋 sign and play to the "Fine" sign
Fine	the end
Marcato	marked, stressed
Moderato	at a moderate pace
Rit.	getting gradually slower
Sim.	continue in a similar way

Dynamics

These tell you how loudly or softly to play.

ff		fortissimo (very loudly)
f		forte (loudly)
mf		mezzo forte (fairly loudly)
mp		mezzo piano (fairly quietly)
p		piano (quietly)
pp		pianissimo (very quietly)
ppp		pianississimo (extremely quietly)
◁	cresc.	get gradually louder
▷	dim.	get gradually quieter

Every effort has been made to trace the copyright holders of the material in this book. If any rights have been omitted, the publishers offer their sincere apologies and will rectify this in any subsequent editions following notification. The publishers are grateful to the following organizations for their contribution and permission to reproduce material.
Backgrounds © 2003 DesignEXchange Company Limited

First published in 2007 by Usborne Publishing Ltd, Usborne House, 83–85 Saffron Hill, London ECIN 8RT, England. www.usborne.com
Copyright © 2007 Usborne Publishing Ltd. The name Usborne and the devices 🐝 🎈 are Trade Marks of Usborne Publishing Ltd.
All rights reserved. No part of this publication may be reproduced, stored in a retrieval system, or transmitted in any form or by any means, electronic, mechanical, photocopying, recording or otherwise, without the prior permission of the publisher.
UE. First printed in America 2007. Printed in China.